DATE DUE			
OCT 4 0 2007			
GAYLORD 234			PRINTED IN U. S. A.

Math in My World

Math in the Car

By William Amato

Welcome Books

Children's Press®
A Division of Scholastic Inc.
New York / Toronto / London / Auckland / Sydney
Mexico City / New Delhi / Hong Kong
Danbury, Connecticut

Photo Credits: Cover and all photos by Maura Boruchow
Contributing Editor: Jennifer Silate
Book Design: Laura Stein

Library of Congress Cataloging-in-Publication Data

Amato, William.
    Math in the car / by William Amato.
        p. cm. — (Math in my world)
    Includes index.
    Summary: Photos and simple text illustrate counting minutes, people, and cars on a trip
to the park.
        ISBN 0-516-23940-6 (lib. bdg.) — ISBN 0-516-23597-4 (pbk.)
            1. Mathematics—Juvenile literature. [1. Mathematics. 2. Counting.] I. Title.

QA40.5 .A528 2002
513—dc21
                                                            2001042355

Contents

My name is Jamal.

My mom and I are going to the park.

Mom **drives** us there.

5

We come to a **stop sign**.

Three people on one **corner** wait to cross the street.

7

Two people on the other corner also wait to cross the street.

How many people will cross?

Five people are crossing the street.

After they cross, we can go.

Mom says we will be at the park by 1:05 P.M.

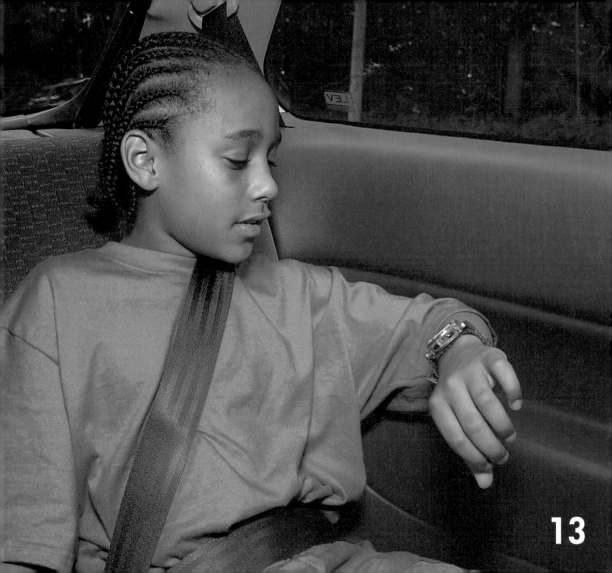

13

It is 1:00 P.M.

How many minutes are left
before we get there?

14

15

There are five minutes left.

I cannot wait!

We are at the park.

Our car is in the **parking lot**.

How many cars are parked here?

19

There are four cars parked here.

We are going to have fun in the park.

21

New Words

corner (**kor**-nur) the place where two streets meet

drives (**drives**) controls the movement of a car

parking lot (**park**-ing **lot**) an area used for parking cars

stop sign (**stop sine**) a red sign that tells drivers to stop for people or cars

To Find Out More

Books

Mega-Fun Math Games: 70 Quick-and-Easy Games to Build Math Skills
by Dr. Michael Schiro
Scholastic Trade

Pigs on the Move: Fun with Math and Travel
by Amy Axelrod
Simon & Schuster Children's Press

Web Site
AAA Math
http://www.aaamath.com
This Web site has lots of math problems and challenging games for all skill levels.

Index

About the Author
William Amato is a teacher and writer living in New York City.

Reading Consultants
Kris Flynn, Coordinator, Small School District Literacy, The San Diego County Office of Education

Shelly Forys, Certified Reading Recovery Specialist, W.J. Zahnow Elementary School, Waterloo, IL

Sue McAdams, Former President of the North Texas Reading Council of the IRA, and Early Literacy Consultant, Dallas, TX